STRANGE but True
CIVIL WAR ☆STORIES☆

By Nancy Clayton
Illustrations by Susan Spellman

LOWELL HOUSE JUVENILE

LOS ANGELES

NTC/Contemporary Publishing Group

For the 19th century storytellers, authors, and poets who were eyewitnesses to the "strange but true" incidents of America's most tragic conflict, and especially for those journalists who recorded the events of that time . . . for children.

—N. C.

Published by Lowell House
A division of NTC/Contemporary Publishing Group, Inc.
4255 West Touhy Avenue, Lincolnwood (Chicago),
Illinois 60646-1975 U.S.A.

Managing Director and Publisher: Jack Artenstein
Director of Publishing Services: Rena Copperman
Editorial Director: Brenda Pope-Ostrow
Director of Juvenile Development: Amy Downing
Designer: Treesha Runnells Vaux

Printed and bound in the United States of America

DHD 10 9 8 7 6 5 4 3 2 1

Library of Congress Cataloging-in-Publication Data

Clayton, Nancy.
    Strange but true Civil War stories / Nancy Clayton.
        p.   cm.
    Summary: Relates true stories from the Civil War, including "Two Skulls Underneath the Tattered Flag," "General Wade Hampton and the Naked Yankee," and "Were They Live Soldiers or Ghosts? You Decide."
    ISBN 0-7373-0110-4 (paper : alk. Paper)
    1. United States—History—Civil War, 1861–1865 Anecdotes Juvenile literature.   [1. United States—History—Civil War, 1861–1865 Anecdotes.]   I. Title.
E655.C53 1999
973.7—dc21
                                        99-23592
                                           CIP

CONTENTS

ACKNOWLEDGMENTS

★

I owe a big thank-you to many wonderful librarians, historians, Civil War researchers, and other knowledgeable folks who helped me complete this book.

I want to thank the editors and staff at Lowell House, including Jessica Oifer and Brenda Pope-Ostrow. A special thank-you to my editor, Amy Downing, for giving me the support and encouragement to start and complete this story collection, and the expertise to see it completed. A special thank-you to my illustrator, Susan Spellman, for her wonderful artwork.

Thank you to my good friend, Professor Jay S. Hoar, University of Maine at Farmington, who provided me with many pages of information.

Thank you to the members of the Sons of Union Veterans, especially Edward T. Maguire in Massachusetts.

I would like to thank the staff at the many university and research libraries who provided assistance, including Mrs. Leo Montandon, reference librarian at Texas Tech University Library; Louise Arnold-Friend and John J. Slonaker, reference librarians at the U.S. Army Military History Institute at Carlisle Barracks, Pennsylvania;

Rebecca Roberts at the University of Alabama Special Collections Library; Peggy Fox at the Harold B. Simpson Research Center, Hill College, Texas; Donald Firsching, Center for American History, Austin, Texas; Donaly E. Brice, Texas State Library; Leah Wood at the U.S. Civil War Center, Louisiana State University; and reference librarians at Southwest Texas State University and the University of Texas at Austin.

A big thank-you to the members of the Texas Division of the Sons of Confederate Veterans and the Texas Marine Department, including Jim Dark, Stephen Lucas, Dr. G. Tom Boyett, John Robinson, and Russell V. Tucker.

I would like to thank Dr. Carolyn Miller at Texas Tech University, and Civil War researchers Michael H. Cumbie (North Carolina), Bill Allen (Wisconsin); and the Texas public school librarians and classroom teachers who let me "bounce" ideas off of them and their students.

Finally, I would like to say how grateful I am for the help and encouragement from two special people—Dr. Judi Repman, Georgia Southern University, for her vast knowledge of children's literature; and my mother—for her love and for feeding my cats when I got lost in the books of the Civil War.

Author's Note

Writing this book has been a wonderful adventure! I spent many fun hours reading through dusty old Civil War storybooks written over 100 years ago. These old histories are full of flowery tales of adventure and bravery.

One of my favorite authors—Washington Davis—wrote a magnificent introduction to one of his story collections that still means so much today: "The history of this war has been written, but the tales of the true bravery of America's noblest sons, with their daring deeds, will ever remain in the hearts of the people, like the traditions of old, become a history of a modern conflict between the brothers of a nation, in which both believed themselves in the right."

I think that is a neat statement. I hope you get excited about the history of our country when you read these strange but true stories. And I hope you will always remember the men and women of both sides, North and South, who sacrificed their lives and property and way of life in a conflict that changed this nation forever.

SNAKES AND SPIDERS OVER FORT PICKENS

★

The first shots of the Civil War were fired on April 12, 1861, at Fort Sumter, South Carolina.

Or were they?

On January 8, 1861, an armed group of Southerners attacked Fort Barrancas, near Pensacola, Florida. The United States forces were in control of three important forts in that area—McRee, Pickens, and Barrancas—and a U.S. Navy yard that protected the Pensacola Harbor. The commander of Fort Barrancas, Lieutenant Adam J. Slemmer, won the fight, but he didn't have enough soldiers to protect all three forts and the yard.

Quickly, he decided to destroy over 20,000 pounds of gunpowder at Fort McRee, disable all of the big guns in Fort Barrancas, and try to move his tiny force of 80 men to Fort Pickens. Pickens was located at the entrance to the harbor and would be the most important of the three to defend.

Two days later, after taking over the abandoned forts, over 500 angry Rebels from Florida, Alabama, and Mississippi, marched to the gates of the navy yard and demanded a surrender. Some of the Yankee officers wanted to surrender, but Lieutenant Slemmer refused. Before he could say another word, one of his own Yankee officers ran to the flag pole and pulled down the United States flag! On that day, January 10, 1861, a United States Navy yard was taken over by the Rebels three months BEFORE Fort Sumter fell!

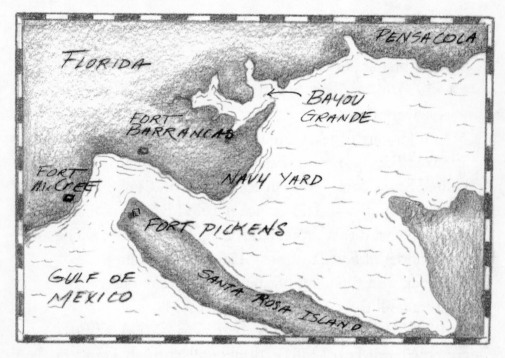

As the Rebels celebrated, Lieutenant Slemmer quickly fled to Fort Pickens with a small band of loyal followers. He was ready for a fight but knew he would have to hold out until President Abraham Lincoln could send rein-forcements. Fort Pickens was a strong fortress that had been built by slaves in the early 1800s. If the Rebels wanted it, they would have to break through its mighty walls made out of 20 million bricks!

Day after day the Rebels demanded surrender, and time after time the answer was no.

One Federal officer, Lieutenant J. L. Worden, tried to pass messages back and forth to the fort. He was caught by the Rebels and thrown into jail on April 15, three days after Fort Sumter was fired on. He became the first prisoner of war.

It took until May for Federal colonel Harvey Brown to sail into the harbor with men and supplies. By November, almost six months later, there were over 7,000 Federal troops, two U.S. war ships, and all of Lieutenant Slemmer's 54-gun battery defending the fort.

After many days of fighting, the U.S. troops took back Fort Barrancas and Fort McRee. Giving up the two smaller forts was a blow to the Rebel fighters, but they still wanted Fort Pickens in order to keep the harbor open to Confederate ships.

People throughout the South demanded more action from the Rebel commander Colonel Braxton Bragg. Newspaper stories, editorials, and well-known speakers pressured the new Confederate government leaders to consider what should be done to win the fort.

Hundreds of suggestions were mailed to newspaper editors calling for more troops, more guns, more ships. Of all the suggestions, one stood out above the rest:

Dear Sirs:

Colonel Bragg should assign a few thousand of his men to a special unit. They should then be sent out across Florida, armed with sacks and small carts. In a short time, these men would be able to gather many loads of diamondback rattlesnakes, canebrake rattlesnakes, pygmy rattlesnakes, copperheads, cottonmouths, and coral snakes. These interesting reptiles could then be loaded into long, thin shells— the kind that fit into the largest of our cannon. These shells could then be fired out and over the fort—and if loaded with care—could be exploded high in the air, then FALL into the fort on top of the Yankees' HEADS!

A word of warning to those who load the reptiles, however. Great care must be taken to see that only the same species are loaded together. Coral snakes with copperheads

just won't do. If different snakes are mixed in the same shell, they might bite each other to death, before having a chance to do their work on the Yankees!

One other suggestion . . . about how to make good use of the corners and little spaces left over inside the shells . . . after the snakes are loaded. Fill each shell with a quart of tarantulas, scorpions, centipedes, and lizards. After all, there is no good reason why every inch of space shouldn't be used—as everyone knows—snakes pack loosely!

It is not known if any of the Confederate leaders actually tried to carry out the "Snake and Spider Plan" on the Federal soldiers. No matter how many suggestions were made or how many plans were tried, the Yankees never surrendered Fort Pickens.

As for Lieutenant Slemmer . . . shortly after the reinforcements arrived, the lieutenant and his men were relieved of duty and sent to New York for a long rest. President Lincoln promoted Lieutenant Slemmer to the rank of major, and then brigadier general. He and all of his men were given special medals for their bravery.

Fort Pickens was restored and used as a military prison after the Civil War. One of its prisoners was the Apache Indian chief Geronimo.

Today the fort is part of the Gulf Islands National Seashore.

Two Skulls Underneath the Tattered Flag

The Battle of Gettysburg was fought on July 1–3, 1864, near the small farm town of Gettysburg, Pennsylvania. In three days of fighting, 23,000 Northern soldiers and 28,000 Southern soldiers were either killed or wounded.

On the third day of fighting, General Robert E. Lee, commander of the Rebel forces, had hoped to split the Federal's line by charging up Cemetery Ridge with General George E. Pickett's brave division. Pickett's Charge, the famous battle mentioned in this story, ended in terrible defeat for the Confederacy. Over 6,500 Rebel soldiers were killed or wounded. Many Rebels were captured—but some were never found.

★

They should be about here. Should be just in front of the stone wall. That's where they fell. Together." The veteran soldier walked slowly through the high grass, holding his small son's hand. He stopped every few feet, bent over, and pushed the grass down to get a closer look at the dirt underneath.

It had been a thousand days since he last walked over this ground. A thousand nights had passed too. Nights filled with dreams of screaming cannon fire, thick smoke, whistling bullets, and waves of voices.

Rebel yells, moans from dying soldiers—both Blue and Gray—crowded into a flashing scene of the young faces and the flag, night after night.

"What were their names, Papa?"

"I never knew, Son," he answered. "I didn't even know they were married, till the night before Pickett's Charge.

"Before Gettysburg, everyone in the regiment thought they were father and son. They joined up together when the Confederacy put out the call to fight for our rights and homes. Come to think of it, I never saw one of them without the other. They pretty much stayed to themselves. Marched, drilled, did their share of the fighting.

"The smaller one, he . . . no, she, I should say, was proud of our flag. Made a special point to make sure it was kept clean and repaired. Did a good job sewing the tears and rips in that flag too. After many a skirmish, she would sit by the campfire till late into the night, sewing it up and making it ready for the next fight, with him sitting beside her.

"That night, after the second day's fighting, they must have felt something bad was going to happen to one or both of them. Just after midnight, I watched as she came up and sat down next to the campfire, took off her soft leather slouch hat, and let her long curls fall down on her uniform coat. First time she'd taken that hat off, as I recall.

"He'd been watching her from the dark. He walked up and sat down beside her. After a while, he reached over and slipped a gold band on her ring finger. She leaned against his side and stared into the fire. Not one man in the outfit said a word. We figured they had their reasons for joinin' the fight and keeping quiet about their being together. Besides, each soldier sittin' around the campfire that night had to settle in their minds what was ahead of them. Takes a lot of quiet to think on such things."

Each time the man stooped to search the grass, his son would hold his breath and close his eyes. "What will they look like, Papa?" he whispered after this particular search ended in plain ground. Opening his eyes again, he continued, "When we find them, I mean."

"Probably won't be much to see, Son. Not after all these months. But we might find just enough to care for. Those awful shells tore up ground enough to cover man and beast. Bodies got covered over in all the confusion, most likely," he sighed.

"We almost broke through the Union line. Remember it was called the High Water Mark—the Angle—the stone wall near the trees?" he said, pointing toward the broken rocks just ahead of them. "General Armistead was leading the way. He and the other commanders started the march with 15,000 of us. Nearly a mile we had to go.

"Sometimes we were 30 men deep in the line. Shot and shell and bullets flying straight at us. Sometimes a wide gap would open up in our moving wall. Ten or more men would fall out. But more from the back and sides would come up and fill in the gap. For a little while longer, we were a moving line again."

"Did they reach the wall, Papa? Tell me again. Did the general really stick his sword through his hat?"

"Yes. They reached the wall. Only about 300 of them. We could see the Angle up ahead, but so many had fallen, we didn't know if we could take it. That's when General Armistead took off his hat, pushed his long sword right up through the middle of its crown, raised it high above his head and shouted, 'Who will follow me?'

"I can't put the words together to tell you how I felt at that moment, Son. All I know is, I've never moved this body the same way again. Seein' that determined general and knowin' we were so close to breakin' through, I couldn't do anything but keep goin' toward the wall."

"Is that when you saw them fall, Papa?"

"I saw him fall first. Took four hits at once. He fell back into her arms. She tried to hold him up, but the force of the bullets coming together that way pushed them both down on the ground. That's when I saw the flag.

"Our color guard officer must have been hit by the same shots. I couldn't see where he fell. All I saw was the flag. Just as she looked up, the flag came falling on top of the both of them. Him, her, and the flag. All on the ground," he said with a glance toward the Angle.

"Well, Son, she didn't even hesitate. She gently let her husband go, grabbed the flag, and in one last burst of life, stood on her feet. She raised the flag as high as she could. I'll never forget it, Son. That's the picture that comes to me when I sleep. Her standing there, her fallen man at her feet, our flag, Armistead waving his hat on the end of his sword, and then . . . "

"Then what, Papa?" whispered the small boy, squeezing his little hand tightly in his father's.

"She fell, Son. The flag fell. Armistead fell. Everything fell that day."

They had come to a small dirt mound covered with dry grass. At first the boy thought it might be a hollowed-out rabbit den. But the man's eye caught the pieces of tattered cloth sticking out of the dirt.

Slowly, he bent down and pulled on one torn edge. Up from the mound came a tattered battle flag. A thousand days of hot sun, rain, cold, and damp had caused the flag to lose its bright colors, but it had done its final duty. Underneath its rotting cloth lay the skulls of the brave young wife and her husband.

"Is this a good place for them, Papa?"

"Yes, Son. This is a good place. It's the place they died together. This should be the place they stay together."

The soldier and his small son quietly dug a small hole under the mound, gently wrapped the skulls in the folds of the battle flag, and buried them in front of the stone wall.

After the 300 Confederates crossed the stone wall, General Armistead was severely wounded and died a short time later. Every single soldier who made it into the Union side was killed, wounded, or taken prisoner.

Dabney's Clothesline Telegraph

When President Abraham Lincoln signed the Emancipation Proclamation in January of 1863, the news spread quickly among black people, especially in Virginia. Thousands of slaves headed toward Union lines and army camps for protection. Many sought work as paid servants and laborers.

Late one night, two escaped slaves—a man named Dabney and his wife—appeared in General Joseph Hooker's Union camp at Falmouth, Virginia, along the banks of the Rappahannock River. Dabney told General Hooker he was a cook and his wife could wash clothes. They had no home and no money and would gladly work for the Yankee soldiers. Hooker agreed to their offer, but little did he know he would be getting much, much more than hot meals and clean laundry in the bargain!

Dabney had never seen a telegraph, a system invented in 1844 for communicating over long distances. One day he asked if he could sit and watch the operator. A young soldier agreed to show Dabney how a telegraph worked and explained how important it was for sending and receiving messages about Confederate troop movements across the river.

Dabney was fascinated! He quickly understood that each series of dots and dashes could be put into words. He listened carefully and watched the young soldier write out the messages.

Late into the night, Dabney sat and told his wife all he had heard and seen in the telegraph tent. By morning, they had decided what they could do to help the Union side.

Dabney's wife went to General Hooker and asked him if she could go back across the river into Confederate territory. She had friends who had told her about a wealthy Southern woman who would pay wages for a much needed laundry servant. She convinced General Hooker she would take the chance of going back into Confederate territory, as she and Dabney needed the money so badly.

Hooker granted her request, and off she went, back across the Rappahannock River.

Within a few days, Dabney could be seen walking down to the north riverbank, standing and looking across to the south bank and slowly going back into General Hooker's tent.

Word soon spread in camp that Dabney was telling Hooker every Confederate troop movement and the whereabouts of every commander in the enemy camp across the river.

This was a great puzzle to the Union officers. Dabney was never seen talking with the scouts or any of the other soldiers. He stayed close to General Hooker's tent—except for his short walks along the riverbank.

And Dabney's reports proved true again and again. Hooker knew which direction the Confederate corps was moving, how long they had been on the march, the numbers in each force, everything about the enemy plans. But how was Dabney getting his information?

Finally, after the officers pleaded with Dabney to share his secret, Dabney took his young telegraph soldier friend to the north riverbank.

From a clearing in the trees, they both looked over the river and into the city of Fredericksburg. Dabney pointed to a little cabin on the outskirts of the Confederate camp, along the south riverbank. He pointed to the clothesline next to the cabin. The young soldier could see wet clothes hanging on the line, drying in the sun.

Dabney explained the clothesline could tell him every plan being made in General Robert E. Lee's headquarters.

Dabney went on to explain how he and his wife had devised their plan to spy on the Confederate headquarters with their own version of the amazing telegraph Dabney had seen that day in the tent.

There was no wealthy Southern lady needing a laundry servant, but there were plenty of high-ranking Confederate officers who had tubs of dirty laundry to wash. Dabney's wife soon had clothes of every color and size to invent her own clothesline telegraph system for Dabney to read on his "walks."

Whenever she heard of a troop movement or a new battle plan, she would hurry to her clothesline and arrange the wet clothes in certain patterns.

A gray shirt was General James Longstreet. When she took it off the line, it meant he was gone to Richmond.

A white shirt was General Ambrose P. Hill. When his army corps moved upstream, she would move the white shirt up to the west end of the clothesline.

The red shirt was General Stonewall Jackson. On this day, the red shirt was down on the right end of the line, so that meant he was at the end of camp, waiting for orders to move.

One day, Dabney and the young soldier watched shirts and underwear move back and forth, and up and down, and back and forth along the clothesline. At last, Dabney's wife took the ends of two blankets and pinned them together at the bottom.

Dabney immediately recognized her message. He ran quickly to the general and explained his wife had made a "fish trap" with the blanket signal. He told Hooker that General Lee was moving all of the units at once. He was trying to draw the Union army into a trap.

Hooker divided his army into two groups. However, before he could catch General Lee, the Rebels rushed westward. Many more battles were to come, but as long as the two great armies were camped across the Rappahannock River, Dabney's clothesline was the fastest and most accurate "telegraph" system General Hooker ever had!

GENERAL WADE HAMPTON AND THE NAKED YANKEE

In the years after the War Between the States, veteran soldiers wrote and published stories about their battle experiences. Many of these story collections are called reminiscences, or memoirs.

In a book called Hampton and His Cavalry in '64, Edward L. Wells wrote of his adventures as a young Confederate cavalry officer under General Wade Hampton. The book, published in 1899, was an instant hit!

One of Wells's stories tells of a strange event one day when General Hampton was returning from a Virginia battle.

The general had ridden a long way that day. He and his horse were tired, and both of them needed a cool drink. From the top of a small rise, he spotted a sparkling stream of water. As far as he could tell, he was alone. He hadn't seen any Federal troops in some time and figured it was safe to ride down to the stream for a quick drink.

He galloped off the rise and down through a clump of small trees to reach the stream bank. As he reached the water's edge, he saw a pile of clothes and a pair of boots and heard water splashing nearby.

Quietly, he pulled his Colt .44 revolver from its leather holster, leaned over the neck of his horse, and slowly moved toward the splashing.

"Well . . . look at that . . . a naked Yankee," General Hampton laughed to himself. "I've never captured a Federal without his britches before. Hands up! Yankee! You're my prisoner."

The startled man leaped up out of the water like a trout catching a fly! He was naked as the day he was born. But he didn't seem concerned about his lack of clothes; after all, he was being taken prisoner by a Confederate.

"Please! Oh, please! Don't take me, sir. I beg you . . . please let me go!" the naked Yankee pleaded. "I'm not even a real soldier. I work for the Quartermaster Department. I'm a simple civil servant, that's all. Why . . . I don't even have a gun or know how to shoot a gun, and I only give out uniforms and supplies and I'm not worth taking prisoner . . . and . . . where did you come from? . . . I thought I would take a nice, refreshing bath, and there aren't supposed to be any Confederates around here . . . "

General Hampton sat on his horse, trying not to laugh out loud, all the time thinking this fellow wouldn't be worth the trouble to take back to headquarters. But the general was so amused at the naked Yankee's begging, he

and his horse just stood there, quietly listening, as the man rambled and rambled all the while in his birthday suit.

Finally, the general spoke. "Well, my fine naked fellow, it seems that you have made a good point . . . or two, or three, or . . . I lost track. And seeing how I don't really have time to listen to any more reasons as to why I should let you go," he said in a long, drawn-out Southern drawl, "my horse and I have decided to let you be on your way."

"Oh! Thank you! Sir!" screamed the naked Yankee. "I'll never trouble you again, and I won't ever bathe here again . . . and I'll just get my clothes . . . and get dressed, and be on my way, and . . ."

"No, no," drawled the general. "Can't let you have the clothes. My men need some good clothes, just like those in that pile. Think of what you gave today as a donation to General Wade Hampton and the men of Hampton's Legion."

The naked Yankee bolted from the water at the words *Wade Hampton*. He ran as fast as he could toward his camp, still naked, splashing and yelling thank-you's all along the stream bank. His last words called out, "I'll name my firstborn son Wade Hampton!"

Many years after that, the general was elected to the United States Senate. One day, as he stepped into a Washington hotel elevator, a young man shouted, "Hold the elevator, please!" He stepped in and stared at the ex-general, Senator Hampton.

"Aren't you General Wade Hampton?"

"Yes," the general answered.

"Do you remember capturing a naked Federal in Virginia during the late war? And . . . do you remember letting him go?"

"Yes!" the general laughed. "I remember that fellow."

"Well, he is my father. My name is Wade Hampton. Good morning, sir!"

With that, the younger Wade Hampton stepped out of the elevator at his floor and went on his way!

THE SINGING BOY WHO SAVED HIS REGIMENT

★

During one of the early battles of Petersburg, Virginia, a Union regiment was in the thick of some of the worst fighting.

Hour after hour they battled the Rebels with all the strength they could muster. At first they were winning. But as the hours dragged on, they started to lose ground. They were exhausted. More and more of them were shot and killed.

Soon they were not moving forward—they were being pushed back!

A burst of shots rang out from the Rebel line! The Union color guard sergeant let out an awful cry.

He was trying to move forward with the flag to reach a high place on the field where all the men would rally round the Stars and Stripes. But the Rebel fire hit him so hard he was nearly cut in two. He crumpled and fell just as he pushed the flag up as high as his arms could reach.

The men of the Union regiment suddenly stopped running and fighting. Like one long wave, they slowly began to creep backward.

Back . . . back . . . they went. They no longer had the heart to fight. It was hopeless. They wept as they backed down from the high point where their sergeant had fallen, next to his flag. It had fluttered down and now lay in neat folds on top of his body.

Officers screamed at the broken line of frightened men. "Keep fighting . . . we can take them . . . don't give up . . . rally round the flag, boys . . . rally round the flag!"

But it was no use to yell at them. It was as if they had lost their hearing. They kept backing up . . . backing up.

Suddenly from the rear of the regiment, a small boy soldier ran to the side of the fallen sergeant. The boy was half the size of the men in his regiment, but that day he was 10 times the size of every man on the field.

He grabbed the flag and scrambled to the high point in front of his fallen comrade. He shouted and lifted the blood-stained Stars and Stripes as high as he could get it above his four-foot frame.

"Rally round the flag, boys! Rally round the flag!" the officers cheered. "Don't desert the colors! The colors, boys, the colors!"

Then, with as clear a voice as was ever heard from the greatest of singers—before or since that day—the small boy began to sing:

> We will rally from the hillside
> We will gather from the plains
> Shouting the Battle Cry of Freedom!

His bright, clear voice carried across the battlefield.

Over the sound of the Rebel guns.

Over the sound of the Union cannon.

Over the sound of the charging cavalry.

It carried across the bodies and across the battle lines. It carried to the headquarters of both sides—to the field hospitals—to Heaven itself!

He sang in such perfect tones, before they realized what they were doing, the regiment joined in with his singing. The men sang the words with new meaning. In perfect pitch and harmony they sang and marched.

Forward! Now walking.

Forward! Now running.

Forward toward the boy and the flag.

The Rebels backed away. The Rebels started to break their lines and run away. In all their confusion, the Rebels could still hear the boy above all the others.

In a matter of minutes, the entire line was swept back from the high point, with the singing boy leading the charge!

A great victory was won for the regiment that afternoon.

And a small boy was made a sergeant that evening.

One of the most popular Union songs, "The Battle Cry of Freedom," was composed by George F. Root in 1862. It was know as a rallying song—a spirit-lifting song for the Union soldiers and their families supporting them. These are the words of the chorus the boy soldier sang that day on the battlefield:

> The Union forever!
>
> Hurrah! Boys! Hurrah!
>
> Down with the traitors,
>
> Up with the stars,
>
> While we rally round the flag, boys
>
> Rally once again
>
> Shouting the Battle Cry of Freedom!

WERE THEY LIVE SOLDIERS OR GHOSTS?

There are many unexplained events that have been observed since the days of the Civil War—over 135 years ago. Accounts of haunted battlefields and strange sightings continue to be reported. This story is about one such incident.

The foreign visitors looked forward to their special tour of Gettysburg National Military Park that day. They had come from around the world to stand on the famous battlefield.

The quiet little Pennsylvania farm town was the scene of three days of terrible fighting in the hot summer of 1863.

They hoped they would be allowed to climb to the summit of Little Round Top, the site of the gallant "bayonet charge" of the 20th Maine. Union colonel Joshua Chamberlain had held the southeastern edge of the hill against a charge of Confederates on July 2, 1863, the second day of the three-day-long battle.

A battlefield guide led the foreign visitors from one famous battle site to another. They walked through the fields of Pickett's Charge and on to the base of Little Round Top. To their great delight, the guide let them climb over the rough boulders and thick underbrush until at last they stood on top of the famous hill.

Unexpectedly, the guide was called back to park headquarters, leaving the group alone on the hill. The visitors didn't mind being left on their own. In fact, they were thrilled to have a little extra time alone on the hill.

From the high point of Little Round Top, they could see many of the most famous battle sites.

"Look there!" exclaimed one excited dignitary. "There! See the Wheat Field, and Devil's Den, and in the valley near the Peach Orchard—soldiers—marching soldiers!"

At once the group turned to see where he was pointing.

"YES! I see them!" shouted one of the visitors.

"Look at that—what precision—what fine marching," said another.

"Indeed so," said another.

Just below them, a regiment of soldiers was drilling and marching in full uniform. They carried Springfield rifles, cartridge belts, knapsacks, bedrolls, canteens—all of the standard Civil War gear.

They marched back and forth just below the hill. The foreign visitors were delighted!

"It must be a special reenactment group the guide has invited for our viewing today," said one.

The visitors cheered and waved to the drilling regiment below.

"Hurrah! Hurrah!" the visitors called out.

"My! Aren't they fantastic! They look so realistic!" said the man who had spotted them first.

"They must have practiced for hours to put on this kind of show," said another.

"I thought these American reenactment groups were just weekend types. You know, a bunch of modern-day men who get together and put on Civil War battle drills. But these fellows are so real," remarked another viewer.

As suddenly as they had appeared, the soldiers turned and marched the old-style quick-march step and silently disappeared into the thick woods.

The visitors applauded and hurried down the hill back to the Visitor's Center. They all agreed they must take time to thank their guide for such a fine display.

When they arrived back at the Visitor's Center, they found the guide and thanked him over and over for the grand show.

"What reenactors?" the puzzled guide asked. "There haven't been any reenactor groups in the park for several days. Come to think of it, you folks are the only visitors we had scheduled. The park has been closed—all day."

GWINE TO TAKE CARE OF YOU

★

Young James Dinkins was too young to join the army when North Carolina seceded from the Union. He had just started his first year as a cadet in a boy's military school when the fighting started. The older students marched off to war, but he had to stay behind.

He pleaded with the headmaster to send for his father. He knew his father would let him go to war. After days of begging for permission to join the army, the headmaster reluctantly sent for James's father.

At last, his father rode up to the front of the school. Following along a few steps behind was old Uncle Freeman, young James's loyal house slave. "He insisted he had to come with me," explained James's father. "Walked all the way. He says if I let you join the army, he will go with you."

James ran from the front porch of the school and hugged both of them at once. "I'm so glad you've come. Father! Uncle Freeman! I must join the fight and do what is right for my new country. You have to let me go. I'm not too young. I'm NOT!" James shouted.

Old Uncle Freeman hung his head. Tears flowed down through his gray beard and onto his tattered cotton shirt.

In his old mind's eye he saw flashes from the past, first of young Massa James wrapped in his first baby blanket. He blinked and saw his young Massa taking his first steps, and then catching his first fish, and then the trail of dust behind his horse as he rode off to military school.

★ ★ ★ ★ ★ ★ ★ ★ ★ ★ ★ ★ ★ ★ ★

Slaves sometimes spoke in their own dialect, or type of speech. Old Uncle Freeman's words **gwine** *and* **Massa** *are the words* **going** *and* **Master**, *respectively. When he calls young James Dinkins "honey," he is saying how much he loves him. The word* **honey** *was used for both boys and girls in Civil War days.*

—N. C.

★ ★ ★ ★ ★ ★ ★ ★ ★ ★ ★ ★ ★ ★ ★

The elderly man straightened up and looked at James eye to eye. "Bless your heart, honey. Your old Uncle Freeman has come to take care of you. Gwine to take care of you as long as old Uncle Freeman lives! GWINE to take care of you."

"We have one war to fight," James's father sighed. "I can't fight another one with you *and* old Freeman against me. You may go, both of you."

Young James Dinkins and Uncle Freeman, his loyal slave, marched off together to join the fighting.

The old man never left the boy's side. He cooked his breakfast. He washed his clothes. He cleaned his tent. He marched with him in drill, and when the time came, fought along side of him in many a battle.

Summer days soon changed and cooler weather came on. James was assigned to another company and found himself sharing a tent so small there was hardly room to turn around.

One cold night, one of James's three tent mates shouted out, "There's not enough room for us and that slave of yours. He can sleep outside from now on."

"No!" James yelled back. "I won't stay in the tent unless Uncle Freeman comes in too. I won't leave him out in this cold weather."

"But you'll freeze out there!" said the others.

"Then we freeze together," James shot back.

After that, not a word was spoken about the matter. Uncle Freeman crawled in and curled up next to young James.

Freeman would get up early every morning and have a warm fire going by the time James and his mates were called to reveille. But old Freeman couldn't keep the winter winds and cold miserable days away from his young Massa and his friends. The boys' uniforms were soon torn and tattered. Their boots were falling apart. Freeman tied strips of cloth to cover the holes and used parts of his old cotton shirt to wrap their feet at night.

The time came when he had no food to cook. The boy soldiers were starving.

One cold morning, James awoke to find Freeman gone. The whole company searched for him. He was nowhere to be found.

James cried. He blamed himself for letting the old slave come with him to war. He must have run away. All these years—Uncle Freeman had cared for him, and his father and grandfather too. He was part of the Dinkins family. How could he run away and leave him?

Two weeks went by and no word. The weather had grown worse. A cold sleet began to fall. James crawled under his blanket and shivered, partly because of the sound of ice hitting the tent and partly knowing his good friend was gone forever.

"BBBRRRRRRR! Who opened that flap!" yelled one of the cadets.

"Who's that? What's going on?"

"Now you hush, honey," whispered the old slave. "Just you see what this here old man has brought his young Massa!"

"Uncle Freeman!" the four of them shouted. "Where have you been? Where did you go?" The boys crowded around the old man, laughing and talking at once. One lit a small candle. The tiny light revealed the face of a tired, half-frozen old black man holding a heavy tow sack.

Uncle Freeman slowly turned the sack upside down and shook its contents onto the tent floor. Fresh rolls of bread, small pieces of ham, candies, cakes, coffee—the likes of which the young soldiers had not seen since their school days. What a wonderful feast! Uncle Freeman had saved them from starvation.

He told his amazing story as they ate. "I knew you couldn't last much longer, and I promised I was gwine to take care of you, young Massa James, so I took off a walkin' to Richmond. Took almost three days . . . and pretty cold, but I got there and I did errands.

"I fed horses, cut wood, carried water, cooked, cleaned boots, just about anything to get enough food in trade. I promised. I promised."

It was only then that James noticed Uncle Freeman's frozen feet. He had lost his shoes, or traded them for food, James would never know which.

Late the next night, after they had all eaten another hot meal, Uncle Freeman died. His trip to Richmond, the cold, and his age had been too much for him.

James Dinkins survived that awful winter and went on to be appointed a lieutenant. After the war he returned to his home in North Carolina.

Years after the war, during every winter when the cold sleet came, James gathered his grandchildren around him and told them the story of old Uncle Freeman.

SAVED BY A BATTLEFIELD SOUVENIR

⭐

James Garrabrant and his brother were members of Company D, 13th New Jersey Regiment. They fought side by side in every battle.

James had the habit of walking through the battlefields and picking up things—souvenirs, he called them—after the fighting was over. His brother would tease him about his souvenir hunting, but it didn't keep James from searching for something unusual or interesting to show everyone back in camp.

During one battle near the Rappahannock, James saw a Rebel soldier shot a few feet in front of him. As the Rebel slumped to the ground, a small, glass-framed daguerreotype, one of the first types of photographs, fell from his pocket.

Now James had never done any of his souvenir hunting during a battle before, but he just couldn't resist. After all, James thought to himself, this Rebel wouldn't be needing the daguerreotype anymore, and it would be a wonderful curiosity to show off in camp that evening.

He quickly bent over, picking up his souvenir without looking at it, unbuttoned his uniform coat, and hurriedly stuffed it inside his upper left coat pocket. There would be plenty of time to examine it later, he thought.

At the very moment he brought his hand out of his coat and grabbed his rifle, he was shot in the chest!

His brother rushed to his side. By the time he got to him, James was flat on his back and motionless. The brother knelt beside him and, gently lifting him up, started searching for the bullet wound.

Frantically, he shouted his name and ripped the buttons as he tore open James's uniform coat. To his amazement, he could find no blood. But there was a gaping bullet hole. A minié ball had definitely hit James in the chest, gone through his coat, and smashed into the daguerreotype!

The brother reached into the upper inside, left coat pocket and pulled out the broken picture. He shook James as hard as he could to try to wake him. After a time, James opened his eyes and tried to take a deep breath. Confused, he looked up at his worried brother. He asked him what had happened and why they were lying on the ground.

Again James tried to take a deep breath but com-plained his chest hurt when he tried to do so. The brother let go of him and fell back laughing so loud, James thought he might be asleep and in the middle of a dream rather than on the battlefield.

The brother finally sat down beside James and handed him the picture. To their disbelief, the minié ball had struck dead center in the framed photo. The ball had hit with such force, it had shattered the glass cover and splintered the wooden back. It had curved out a deep groove inside the plate itself and was still sitting there. If it had not been for the soft copper plate stopping it, that bullet would have gone straight into James's heart!

That night, as the men of the 13th Regiment sat around the campfire, James rubbed his bruised chest and finally pulled out the picture and bullet to take a closer look at his latest battlefield "souvenirs."

After studying them for a long moment, James turned to his friends and announced he had been saved from certain death by the face of a pretty Southern girl!

The daguerreotype (pronounced duh-GEH-roh-type) was the most common type of picture taken during the Civil War. Images appeared in a half hour on chemical-covered, silver-coated copper plates that were exposed to sunlight. The process was invented by Louis Daguerre in 1837. He and Joseph Niépce, another scientist in France, were the fathers of modern photography. Thanks to their invention of the daguerreotype, the Civil War was the first war to be photographed from beginning to end.

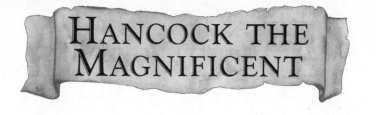

HANCOCK THE MAGNIFICENT

★

*Both Confederate and Union armies relied on information
gathered by scouts and spies. Sometimes, these brave men and
women were caught and sent to military prisons. Hancock,
one of General Ulysses S. Grant's Union scouts, was arrested,
but the Confederates just couldn't keep him in prison.*

★

L ate in the war, a company of Confederate soldiers
captured Hancock and sent him to Castle Thunder
Prison in Richmond, Virginia.

He was a happy-go-lucky sort of fellow. He entertained
his cell mates with songs, jokes, dances, and funny faces.

One evening, right in the middle of a song, he suddenly
stopped, threw up his hands, weaved around the cell, and
fell flat on his stomach like a sack of cement to the floor.

The prisoners yelled for the guards.

"He's dead! He's dead! Poor fellow."

"Make way . . . make way!" the guards rushed in
shouting.

The prison surgeon was called to see if he were really dead or had just fainted. As it happened that evening, the surgeon had just returned from a long, cold ride and was in a hurry to get to supper.

He leaned over poor Hancock. He didn't really examine him and announced to the startled group, "Dead."

In less than 20 minutes Hancock was carried from the cell, laid in the back of the hospital wagon, and driven out of the prison to the burial spot.

When the driver reached the burial grounds, he walked to the back of wagon and found the body gone!

Thinking he might have bounced Hancock out of the wagon on the rough journey, he drove back along the way he came and stopped from time to time asking several pedestrians, "Hey! Seen a corpse anywhere?"

No Hancock!

Hancock was a tricky scout. He had planned this trip from the start. He had dropped out of the wagon about halfway from the prison and joined the pedestrians walking along the road. He knew he would be picked up by a patrol if he stayed in the woods or on the road. His best chance to slip past the driver was to blend in with the local people.

Hancock was always ready for any emergency. He had sewn money in the lining of his vest, and he simply walked straight into town and up to the front desk of the finest hotel. There, Hancock registered as a guest from Georgia and spent a most restful night.

The next morning he roamed around town, acting as if nothing were unusual. He purchased a new set of clothes and ate in the finest dining room. But after lunch, he ran head-on into a squad of soldiers who had his description—or so they thought!

Poor Hancock. It seemed as if he wouldn't escape this time. But just as the soldiers put their hands on him, his eyes crossed and his mouth drew down to the left side.

He fumbled and mumbled and called for the hotel clerk to verify he was a "visitor from Georgia." He made such a scene, the hotel clerk insisted he was no Yankee scout and the squad should leave him alone.

The soldiers let go of him, and he walked calmly down the street. Free again!

Hancock's one weakness was his love of spending. In four days all of his money was gone. He was standing in the post office when the wagon driver spotted him.

"Dead man! Got you now!"

This time Hancock drew his mouth up to the right, pulled his left eye down, and pretended to be deaf. The wagon driver wasn't so sure when he saw that twisted face, but he wasn't about to be fooled again. He ushered Hancock out the door and down the street, back to prison.

Hancock's face was so twisted and his acting so believable, the prison guards were confused. They couldn't say it was Hancock for sure!

They brought in his cell mates and asked them to identify him. They were confused too. No one could tell

if this poor creature, with his twisted mouth and droopy eye, was really Hancock.

For seven long days and nights Hancock the scout kept his mouth pulled up to the right, his left eye pulled down to the left, and pretended he couldn't hear a word that was said.

But on the eighth day, he grew tired of his trick and yawned and stretched and returned his face to its happy look.

The minute he relaxed, he was instantly recognized by both the prisoners and guards.

The Confederates were amazed by his nerves of steel and perseverance. They decided to keep him under close watch until a firing squad could be formed to shoot him as a spy.

But once more, the crafty Hancock won out.

The war ended just 10 days before he was to stand in front of the squad!

He walked out of Castle Thunder Prison a free man.

500 BULLETS

The soldiers who loaded and fired cannons were members of the artillery. One of the most common cannons used by North and South was the 12-pound Napoleon howitzer. Weighing about 2,500 pounds, it was set on a frame between two large wagon wheels and pulled from battlefield to battlefield by a team of four to six horses. A seven-man crew loading and firing solid shot as fast as twice a minute could hit their target up to 2,000 yards—that's as far as 20 football fields away!

The gunner was the head of each crew. It was his job to make sure his piece was in place and ready to fire as part of a battery. In the early part of the Civil War, there were six cannons in a battery, and in some battles there were as many as eight batteries firing at one time!

During the Battle of Second Bull Run (or Second Manassas, as Confederates called it), there was one brave Union gunner who was determined to save his Napoleon— no matter how many bullets were fired at him.

Move that cannon in here! NOW!" shouted the gunner. "And don't bother unhitching those grays. We may need to move fast if Stonewall Jackson breaks through."

The late afternoon air was already thick with gunfire and smoke from the first round of fighting. The gunner's crew was frantic. He was shouting orders to them as fast as the bullets were flying.

"Sponge that piece clean this time. I don't want any misfirings. And get those boxes of ammunition in line. It won't be long now, boys."

Just as he said that last word, a screaming Texas brigade charged up Henry Hill, also known as Henry House Hill.

The Union front line ran toward the turnpike to get away. The Rebels would surely take the strong point and destroy the gunner's six Napoleon cannons. They had to hold the hill.

"NO! You're not taking my gun! We can't lose all the guns. NO!" screamed the gunner, shaking his fist at the Rebels. He ran to the front of his gun and jumped straight into the path of a galloping Rebel cavalryman. The Rebel jerked on his horse's reins, trying to swing around and knock the gunner down. But the gunner leaped at the Rebel and grabbed for the reins. They flew in a circle of dirt, reins, hands, and sword until the gunner finally got hold of the Rebel's arm. He pulled as hard as he could and yanked the man head over heels out of the saddle. In one swift jump, the gunner landed hard in the saddle.

Once on the horse, the gunner spun around and headed for his gun. The four grays seemed to sense what was coming next. They had already bolted from the noise of the charge and had run right up to the gunner and his mount! The gunner reached for the leather strap hanging off the lead horse. In a cloud of dust and gun smoke they were off!

But where could they go? Where could they take the cannon? The Rebel infantry was on their left. The remains of the Rebel cavalry was behind them. And now, a four-foot ditch was right in front of them!

The ditch ran the whole length of the valley. It was not only too deep for a team of horses, it was also too wide to jump with a team hitched to a 12-pound cannon. The only way out was to run along the edge of the ditch—over a mile—go around it, and then up a small rise to safety.

The company of Confederates on the gunner's left began a terrible hail of bullets. But the gunner was flying through the lead. The grays were straining and panting and stretching every muscle to keep up with their screaming master and the enemy's steed.

"Fire! Fire! More ammunition! Aim lower . . . aim at the horses . . . fire at the horses!" yelled a Rebel officer as he rode back and forth behind the company of Rebel infantry. "Bring me the best shooters in the company."

One man stepped forward. He was known as the finest marksman in the outfit. "Bring him a box of cartridges. The rest of you keep shooting!" said the officer.

"But, sir! We've used near 500 bullets and can't bring him down! Look at him, sir . . . " one amazed Rebel shouted out, standing up and pointing to the racing cannon.

The officer ignored him. "Keep firing! That's an order!"

The Rebel marksman loaded his Enfield rifle, stretched out on the dirt, and took dead-eye aim on the gunner.

He fired.

One of the grays screamed in pain, threw his head back, and briefly stumbled. But to the marksman's surprise and the dismay of the officer, the gray kept on running.

Again and again the marksman loaded, aimed, and fired. One at a time, he put a paper cartridge in his mouth and tore it open with his hand, poured the gunpowder deep inside the barrel, and rammed the bullet and powder in with his ramrod. He quickly cocked the hammer halfway back, placed a percussion cap in place, pulled to a full cock, aimed, and fired.

He shot his gun until the barrel was so hot, it burned the tips of his fingers. His mouth and lips were black from the dozens of cartridges he had torn open.

Onward! Onward!

The gunner at last reached the end of the ditch. Finally, he was out of range of the Rebel marksman. The grays pulled the gun to the top of the rise—to safety—and the gunner yelled for his comrades to come for the prize.

But the gunner didn't go with the grays. Instead, he pulled on the reins of the Rebel stallion until the horse stood straight up on his hind legs. He waved with his hat and cheered for one long second at the marksman and his mates who tried so hard to bring him down.

They couldn't hear what he shouted, but without hesitation, the entire company of Rebels rose to their feet and returned a thundering cheer of their own—a shout of respect for the brave gunner.

As the Rebel Yell was fading, one last cheer of respect came from the marksman. Until that day, he had never missed his mark.

THE GHOST OF CHECKPOINT 12

Each Federal army fort or camp was guarded day and night by soldiers. Visitors and traveling soldiers had to go through "checkpoints" where they had to show a pass or proper papers or give a reason for being in the area.

There had never been any problems at one such guard-house, known as Checkpoint 12, until the morning the day officer heard all the yelling about a ghost.

"Come, come, young man. Now slow down and tell me exactly what you saw."

"'Twere a ghost, sir! It really were a GHOST!" quaked the private. The officer of the day was trying to calm down the shaking private who was on guard duty that morning.

"Get a hold, man! There are no such things as ghosts. Your duty is to guard this checkpoint and watch for Rebel spies."

"I tell the truth, sir, as my dear old mama raised me, 'twere a ghost, sir, a floatin' right past my checkpoint."

The officer of the day looked the young Irishman up and down. The private's face was so pale, it made his red hair stand out like a campfire burning at midnight.

"Now . . . now," the officer said in a calming tone, "start again, and tell me what you saw—or think you saw—and explain why you let 'it' . . . or who . . . or whatever, get past this checkpoint."

The private took a quick breath and started again. "'Twere a ghost. It came a floatin' out of the hillside, over there, against the graveyard. It walked right across the graves—stopped and looked straight at me. It shook its fist at me. It kept on a walkin' and walkin' right into that bush—that one next to the fort. Then it disappeared EN-TIRE-LEE!"

"In the bush? Disappeared in the bush?"

"Yes! Sir! It melted away, melted into air. 'Twere floatin' along, but I saw it melt into the bush. 'Twere tall—mighty tall—and dressed in white, an awful sight with eyes all o' fire!"

The officer turned and walked up the hill toward the graveyard. The private crept along close behind. As they walked, the officer scanned the rocky ground for footprints. He figured this "ghost" might be a Rebel in a bedsheet, trying to sneak into the fort. But he couldn't figure how this Rebel was able to melt into the bush. And he had never seen one with "eyes o' fire" before.

"Buy my pies and cakes, sir? Fresh pies and cakes for the brave lads?" a hoarse woman's voice suddenly whispered behind the men.

"Saints preserve us!" screamed the two men as they whirled around to face a tall, scraggly old woman. Her face was hidden under a white bonnet. She was standing almost on top of them, holding a small basket under one arm, and trying to keep a flowing white shawl wrapped around her shoulders.

"Where did you come from, woman?" yelled the officer, quite shaken.

"I come to sell my pies and cakes and see my man who is serving with the 14th Maryland. Do you know him?"

The officer cut her off. "NO! I don't know him. I don't want any pies or cakes. And where did you come from just now? Where is your pass? This is Federal Checkpoint 12! How is it you made no sound walking up behind us in this rocky graveyard? Show me your pass."

The private was hugging the officer now. "Sir, look at her eyes. And look to see if she has a pair o' feet."

The officer leaned forward and strained to get a close look inside the bonnet, but his eyes fell to her feet instead.

Boots. Men's boots. Why would a woman be wearing men's boots, and why wouldn't they have heard her walking?

The woman followed the officer's eyes, and before he could speak, she said, "My man give me his fine boots,

★ 69 ★

don't you see? Been so cold and all." She dropped her head to her chest before the officer could get a look at her face.

The officer wasn't satisfied with that answer. He told her she had to come with them to the fort. She refused to move. She kept insisting she was only a poor woman selling her pies and cakes.

At last she convinced the officer she had friends who lived just behind the fort, down the road a little way off. They would tell the men she was just a poor woman who made her living selling her pastries.

Up the hill, through the graveyard, and behind the fort walked the woman, the officer, and the private.

That was about eleven-thirty in the morning.

Noon came, and no guard or officer of the day reported back to the fort from Checkpoint 12.

One o'clock, and no guard or officer.

Two o'clock, and the regimental commander sent a squadron of cavalry to search for the missing private and officer.

Up the hill, through the graveyard, and behind the fort—galloped the cavalry.

Three o'clock and no word of the private, the officer, or the squadron. Word spread through the regiment that a full search must be made. Assembly was sounded!

Suddenly, the cavalry returned at full speed. The regiment stood in silence, watching as the cavalry officer jumped from his horse and raced into the commander's office.

In less than a minute the commander came out and stood in front of the regiment, holding a crumpled sheet of paper.

"Men! We have word of our missing comrades! Please listen as I read from this crude writing found stuck in one of the graveyard markers on the other side of the hill. Our comrades are being held by a Rebel. I can't quite make out the end of the note, but it seems to be signed by a Rebel officer, a Lieutenant Bland."

Commander of the fort,
I have captured your officer and a private. In exchange, I have a basket of pies and cakes I would like to keep. I came upon them holding said pastries and a woman's white shawl. They keep muttering something about a . . .
Come quickly.
Lt. Bland, Confederate Army

"Hurry!" yelled the commander. The entire regiment marched out to find the private and the officer, the mysterious white shawl, and Rebel lieutenant Bland.

Up the hill, through the graveyard, and behind the fort—marched the regiment.

They rushed to the spot where the note was found, but their search until dark was in vain.

The private, the officer, the white shawl, Rebel lieutenant Bland, the basket of pies and cakes, AND the ghost of Checkpoint 12—were never seen again!

★ ★ ★ ★ ★ ★ ★ ★ ★ ★ ★ ★ ★ ★ ★

What really happened to the people in this story? Nobody knows for sure, but I think Lieutenant Bland came upon the strange woman and the two soldiers and took all three of them back to his Confederate camp. But he carefully worded his note to create a real mystery.

Why? Because I believe the "ghost" was really a lady spy. After the lieutenant left the note describing a white shawl, the lady knew the Federal soldiers would be looking for her. I think she probably moved to another fort. Lieutenant Bland was told not to tell anyone about her activities, and to keep them quiet, the two Federal soldiers ended up in a Rebel prison for the rest of the war.

—N. C.

★ ★ ★ ★ ★ ★ ★ ★ ★ ★ ★ ★ ★ ★ ★

NINE LIVES AND THREE NAMES

There are many amazing stories of brave drummer boys who marched off to fight for North and South. Little boys as young as age six played the drum calls that woke the men, marched them to breakfast, drilled them, and charged them into battle.

Hundreds of boys changed their names or told fibs about their ages just for a chance to sign up and join the fight. We will never know just how many boy soldiers were part of the Civil War or what some of their real names were.

But we do know the truth about one young drummer boy and the true story of how his name was changed by nine wounds and a proud regiment!

★

Columbus Washington Reinhardt was born near Columbus, Tennessee, on March 1, 1845. He liked his name, because it always told everyone who met him where he was from!

By the time the Civil War started in April 1861, he had just turned 16. He traveled to Fort Gaines, Alabama, and reported to the recruiting office to join the Confederate Army.

At first, the old sergeant took one look at Columbus Washington and remarked, "Son, you look mighty young and puny to join this regiment. Just how much do you weigh?"

"All of 72 pounds, sir!" snapped Columbus Washington.

"Seventy-two pounds! Why, I have an old hound dog that weighs more than you do. Columbus Washington, indeed. We're signin' up MEN today. You man enough to do your part?" the crusty sergeant sneered.

"I 'spect I'm man enough for this outfit and besides, I hear you need a drummer. I can learn and I can move fast and I can lead the men in a charge, and—"

The sergeant interrupted him, "All right! But there's just one thing, how's about we shorten that name of yours? How does 'C. W.' sound? C. W. the Drummer Boy of the 25th Alabama Infantry Regiment!"

Columbus Washington cheered! He had a new home, a new name, and an important job to play the army drum calls for the 25th Alabama.

C. W. marched off to war and was soon playing his drum in battle after battle. His regiment was moved to join other brigades and divisions, and he drummed for many famous units: Gladden's Brigade, Withers's

Division, Polk's Corps. Most all of them heard C. W. drum for his 25th Alabama.

He was light on his feet. He could run fast and dodge charging cavalry. In one battle, a cannonball just missed landing on top of him!

C. W. took part in every battle his regiment was in—except for the *nine* times he was wounded and had to undergo emergency operations!

He was shot in the head at the Battle of Shiloh.

He was shot in the ankle at the Battle of Murfreesboro.

He was wounded in the eye at Missionary Ridge.

He caught a bullet in his belt buckle at the Battle of Chickamauga.

In one battle, a soldier raced up to him and hit him on the head and shoulders with the butt of a Springfield rifle!

During a thrilling charge, he ran up to the top of a hill, only to come face to face with an enemy soldier. The soldier stabbed at him with an 18-inch steel-tipped bayonet—catching him in the side.

C. W. had earned quite a name for himself. One of his friends remarked, "You've had six hits. Three more and your nine lives are used up! Just like a house cat . . . nine lives is all you got. Be careful, 'cause you're the only drummer boy in the regiment."

A short time later, during the Battle of Resaca, an enemy sharpshooter hit C. W. in the knee. He limped back to the field hospital to have his knee tended, but on the way was captured by troopers from Wilson's Cavalry.

On the way back to the Federal lines, he and several other wounded comrades escaped! They crawled a hundred feet down to a stream and met up with another troop of Wilson's men. Captured again!

C. W. asked one of the guards if he could get a drink from the stream.

"My knee hurts awful bad . . . and I'm so thirsty. Just let me wash my leg off?" he asked a trooper.

"Make it quick, drummer boy."

No sooner had C. W. stepped into the water than he was off like a bullfrog. He splashed and thrashed and hopped from one rock to another, dodging bullets and his captors, till he finally reached the other bank.

He walked, ran, stumbled, and ended up crawling all night long until he reached the 25th Alabama—safe but hurting—with his right knee swollen bigger than his head!

The colonel of the 25th Alabama looked at him that morning and sighed, "What a victorious escapade for a drummer boy! A true victory! That's who you are—the victor! VICTOR—the Drummer Boy of the 25th Regiment!"

C. W. was no longer Columbus Washington or C. W. to his men or his family. When word reached his home in Tennessee about his daring escape and his seven wounds, his father went to the county courthouse and had his son's name changed to Victor. Victor Reinhardt.

It was some time later when his father heard about two more close calls for Victor. During the famous Battle of Atlanta, Victor was shot in the right leg.

Then, in one of his final battles, a Yankee cavalry officer charged at him during a fierce battle at Franklin and sliced Victor's left arm with a sword.

Victor came home in 1865 with nine battle wounds, three names, and the respect of his beloved 25th Alabama Infantry Regiment.

THE LAST COW IN THE COUNTY

Hans was only 16, but he knew how to take care of himself. He had been a Yankee soldier long enough to pick up some good business sense along the way. When coffee was worth more than bullets, he'd made a few trades with the Rebels. He knew how to make a few dollars on the side, especially when a good business deal came along.

All of his experiences came in handy the day he and a few fellow soldiers found a nice fat spotted cow grazing alone in a quiet field.

Ssshhh . . . don't spook her, boys," whispered Hans. "Yummm . . . YUM! I can taste those T-bones already," one of the soldiers whispered back. "It's been so long since I had fresh meat, well, I can't remember when I had fresh meat. When DID I have fresh meat last, Hans?"

"SSSHHHH! Quiet! You won't get nothin' but the smell of runnin' scared cow feet, 'less you stay still till I shoot her!" Hans snapped back. He carefully aimed his rifle, squeezed the trigger, and KA-BOOM!

Everyone in camp enjoyed the hot steaks that evening and well into the next day. When it came time to do something with the spotted cowhide, Hans stepped up and said, "I figure that spotted hide's mine, boys. I donated the bullet and did the shootin' and I got plans for those spots."

They all agreed he was entitled to the hide, mainly because their stomachs were full for the first time in weeks, thanks to his good shooting. Most of the soldiers thought Hans was going to make a nice coat for himself, or maybe a new leather mat to go under his blanket. But Hans, the businessman, had bigger plans.

On their march through Georgia, he remembered how the civilians talked about hides being so scarce. He also knew there was a local tannery about a mile from camp. Leather and fresh hides were bringing money into the South right about then, and he was going to get more out of this spotted cow than a couple of steaks.

He scraped and cleaned the spotted hide as best he could, rolled it up in a tight bundle, tied it with rope, mounted his horse, and rode off to the tannery.

At first, the shopkeeper was glad to see Hans and his bundle. "Got a fresh hide there, son?" he asked Hans.

"Yep. Fine hide. Hear you Southerners are paying top dollar for good hides. Need a good fresh hide?"

"Why, yes! Yes! I need a good fresh hide," the excited shopkeeper answered. "Let me see what you've got.

Hides are bringing three dollars. Roll it out and let's take a look."

Hans stepped back and untied the rope. With a big WHOOSH, the spotted cowhide spread out till it nearly covered the shopkeeper's entire floor.

"What do you give me?" Hans asked, waiting for the surprised man to speak.

"RAT TAILS AND SWAMP RATS!! YOU YAN-KEE THIEF! You've gone and shot my old spotted cow! The LAST cow I had! The LAST cow in this county! MY OWN COW!" The shopkeeper was jumping up and down so hard the floor was shaking. His face was turning bright red, and the more he jumped and the louder he shouted, the more his eyes popped out. Hans thought the man would surely explode!

"You Yankee! You Yankee! You shoot my OWN cow and then bring the hide in here to sell it to me! My own cow! You want me to buy my own hide! OUT! OUT! Get out of my shop!"

The shopkeeper reached down to roll up the spotted cowhide, when Hans stepped up and put his foot on the end nearest to him. The shopkeeper looked up at Hans's black cavalry boot and glared at him.

"Take your hands off. Off! Now maybe this here cow was yours, I don't know that for sure, and not much left of it to tell true, but I DO know it's mine now. You can't have this here hide till you pay me three dollar. Three dollar . . . that's what you said, when me and this hide walked in the door. You pay up or I'll shoot you a-standin' here!"

It didn't take long for the shopkeeper to make up his mind about the situation. With a whole troop of Yankee cavalry camped just down the road and this young fellow standing there with a loaded rifle in his hand, he stood up and stomped to his desk. He pulled three dollars out of the tin cash box and paid Hans for "their" hide!

BABY ON THE BATTLEFIELD

★

O ur regiment was told the battle would be fierce that day. We were ready for them . . . no matter what they might try. Our cavalry rode out first. The battery, or group of cannons, had been giving them heck all morning and we thought we could take the field by noon at the latest.

A couple of scouts reported there might be civilians nearby. There were a couple of abandoned farm houses on the edges of the battlefield, but as far as the scouts could determine, no women or children were left in the area. There had been earlier reports of a woman and her kids somewhere, but the scouts didn't make mention of them to the officers.

I had my Enfield rifle loaded, my cartridge box strapped on, and had filled my canteen before the cavalry rode through. My tent mates were ready too. Seemed like we were all awake before the drummer boy played the first call. I guess we were restless, day of the big battle and all.

We lined up just like we drilled. We had practiced for hours on how to stand at attention and move our guns from our sides to our shoulders. They called it coming to order arms and shouldering arms. We listened for the forward march call.

And we were ready.

It seemed like only a minute till the cavalry was off and out of sight. We cheered when they galloped off the side of the line—them whooping and hollering back at us. Before I knew it, the drummer was playing "Charge." The colonel was screaming "Forward!" and we all moved like a great ocean wave across that old cornfield.

I was moving forward, but I don't remember my feet actually walking. My heart was racing. I was sweating hard and was breathing like I'd been running a long time.

Shots! Bullets whizzed by my head. I felt a tug on my coat sleeve and saw the man next to me fall backward. I saw his feet fly up, and then I felt something wet on my back. I held onto my rifle with my left hand, rubbed my right hand across my shoulder, and when I brought it back to grab my rifle, I saw bright, red blood. That's the first time I saw blood on a battlefield.

I kept moving. I don't know what happened to that fellow who flew behind me. By this time, bullets were everywhere. The smoke was so darned thick I could hardly see anything in front of me.

I heard the colonel yell, "Get down . . . keep firing!"

I threw myself flat out on the ground, so hard I almost lost my rifle.

That's when I saw him—a baby boy was crawling along like he was on a Sunday picnic. Cone-shaped bullets, minié balls, flew in all directions, and he wasn't crying or calling out. Just crawling.

A couple of our cavalry riders were headed straight for him. They couldn't possibly see him through the smoke and shelling. He was too low to the ground, and no one in his right mind would ever expect to see such a sight, not in such a place, on such a day.

I jumped up, leaving my rifle. I half ran and half crawled toward him. A cannon shell exploded right behind him. I had about 10 feet to go when one of the cavalrymen appeared to have spotted him. He was heading straight for the boy, but something was wrong. The horse's eyes were closed. Blood covered its head and was dripping off the reins. The rider had also been shot, lifeless in the saddle. Death was on a collision course with that sweet little baby boy. I made one final jump toward the baby, pushing off the ground like a frog leaping from a lily pad to a swamp fly. I landed square on him, cradling him as I hit. Together we tumbled, over and over and over, out of the way of the horse and the unconscious rider. The trunk of a tree stopped our roll. I watched the horse and rider disappear into the smoke.

Then the baby started crying. After all that shooting and smoke and blood, I went and made him cry!

I laughed so hard at his tears, I fell over. Pretty soon we both grew quiet. He grinned up at me and I grinned back. "Wait till the men in the 14th Regiment see you," I whispered to him.

Our side won that day, but I felt like I had a personal victory too. I came walking into camp with my prize sitting on my shoulders, little feet dangling on either side of my grinning head, and yelled out, "Come see what I found on the battlefield!"

We called him our "Child of the Regiment" and figured we would adopt him—make him a mascot or tiny drummer boy or something. He reminded us of what we were in this for. He was a link to home and the men who had little ones like him, waiting for them, after the terrible fighting was over.

We sat by the campfire and listened to him laugh. As the fire burned down to embers, we talked quietly of home.

That pleasant night passed too quickly. With the drummer's first call came the sounds of a weeping woman. She appeared on the edge of camp.

"My baby! My baby!" she cried. "Have you seen my little blue-eyed baby? We were trying to cross the cornfield when the battle started, and he crawled away from me. Oh! Please! Have you seen my baby?"

I flinched as I heard her. I knew he would be safe, but when I placed him in her arms, my heart broke. She cried and hugged him so close, I thought she would squeeze the life out of him for sure.

The whole regiment gathered around and watched as she kneeled down, still clinging to her boy. She bowed her head and prayed for us.

She thanked us. The enemy.

TRAPPED IN HIS COAT

The Confederate officers in the Army of Northern Virginia wore long gray coats. These "frock coats" were made of heavy wool. Most of them hung down almost to a man's knees! In the hot, humid summers of the South, the soldiers were miserable in them. But as hot and sweaty as they got, they couldn't complain in front of their men. They were the leaders! They had to set a good example.

Did they ever think about shortening the frocks or throwing them away altogether? One young officer was asking himself those very questions one hot afternoon, but a strange incident made him change his mind.

He was so tired. He had marched and fought for days. He was sunburned and dirty—and hungry, especially. His regiment had been cut off from their supply wagons, and none of them had eaten in two days.

He called the men to a halt and told them to search for food in the woods nearby. Everyone scattered in all directions. The sight and sound of several hundred hungry men running through the woods and yelling at the top of their lungs would surely rustle up some tasty critters soon!

He was too tired, though. He couldn't keep up. His legs were aching. He bent over, trying to get his breath.

"Forget this!" he gasped out loud.

He stumbled toward a large tree on the edge of the woods. He plopped down so hard he caused a small shower of leaves to shake loose and cover his frock coat.

He gave a great sigh of relief and closed his eyes as he leaned back against the trunk. He thought of home, and he thought of supper. He tried to remember the smell of homemade biscuits and baked ham and sweet potato pie. He was tired of the fighting and longed for a good meal and a chance to get out of his sweaty long coat. He wondered what it would be like to march without it. For two bits, he would gladly cut off the tails—or better yet— throw it away.

He unbuttoned it and threw it wide open. But in his haste to sit down and rest, he had somehow tangled the ends. Where before they lay next to his legs, the folds of gray wool now stuck out on either side of him. From the front, it must have looked as if there were little tents under each arm!

Cooler now, he was just about to drift off to sleep when he heard the voices of his men getting closer and closer to his tree. They were screaming something about a rabbit.

"Thar she is! Thar she is!"

"No! I got her now!"

"She's mine! Rabbit stew tonight, boys!"

The little rabbit dashed from tree to tree, over rocks, around little bushes, and just steps ahead of the hungry men.

The soldiers were running and jumping and yelling at that rabbit. They looked like wild hares themselves, the way they were chasing that quick little critter!

They were screaming the Rebel Yell and having a grand time. He wondered how they could have that much energy after two days without food. He laughed out loud when he imagined that rabbit in a pot—being watched by a couple of hundred starving soldiers!

He sat up straighter, because the men were getting closer to his resting spot. Over to his right, one tripped over a rock and crashed, causing about a half a dozen others to fall over him and crash too!

As he glanced toward his left, he spotted the rabbit. It was racing frantically right toward him! Just then, that rabbit spied one of the little tent folds in the frock coat. It lunged straight ahead in one huge leap—a good 15 feet—right into the dark opening, under his left arm!

In all the confusion of the rock crash, the men had failed to see where the rabbit went. They were trying to pick themselves up and run at the same time, which made them fall all over each other, again and again.

"I see her! I see her!" someone on the bottom of the pile shouted. But it wasn't her at all. In all of the confusion, they had failed to see another soldier who had come crawling through the thick brush—causing the tall grass to move ahead of him!

They all took off running toward the shaking grass, yelling again, and soon disappeared into the woods.

He clutched his coat with glee.

Food at last!

Keeping that long coat *on* was worth it after all!

Back from the Dead and Gone Again

The Battle of Chickamauga cost the Union 16,000 dead and wounded soldiers. The Confederate forces suffered the loss of over 18,000. From the 20th Georgia Regiment, 17 of the 23 officers were killed, while the 22nd Alabama lost over half of its men and half of its officers in one day alone.

In the confusion of this terrible fight, many men were never accounted for. Some were blown to pieces by cannon fire, while others simply disappeared. Years after Chickamauga, one Union general was still wrestling with his memory of one such lost soldier.

It can't be him!" General Horace Porter whispered to himself as he passed by the fine-looking gentleman in the hotel lobby. It had been 20 years since the Civil War.

"I'm seeing a ghost," he muttered softly.

The retired Union general turned and stared at the man. He felt uneasy. A quick chill ran through his chest. He walked through the lobby and into the hotel dining room. He spotted a table in the far corner of the room. Rushing to it, he pulled one of the chairs around to sit with his back to the wall, and almost fell into it in his rush to sit down. From this position he could study the man from a distance and try to bring himself to remember that awful day during the Battle of Chickamauga.

In August of 1863, General William S. Rosecrans and the Federal Army of the Cumberland were adding new recruits. They had a big fight coming and needed at least 60,000 men to do the job.

President Lincoln had ordered his generals to take control of the rail center at Chattanooga. It was the most important transportation center of the South. Whoever controlled Chattanooga held the route to the heart of the Confederacy.

In order to succeed, Rosecrans's army would have to battle the fierce Confederate leader—General Braxton Bragg—and his 66,000 Rebels on the banks of Chickamauga Creek.

A month before the battle, a new Union cavalry recruit rode into General Porter's camp. He was all of age 12 . . . if that old.

The picture of that short, pale-faced boy soldier flashed through the old general's mind.

"Robbing the cradle . . . babies from the nursery gone to war," he remembered.

He wondered then, as he did now, why the recruiters would sign up such youngsters for cavalry duty. He could

only suppose there were not enough men, and underage boys like this one were fearless.

The general remembered how the troop adopted the new recruit as their mascot. He was given army papers to carry, fed the horses, watered the general's fine stallion, and would stay near headquarters to hold the reins of visiting officers' mounts.

When the battle started on September 18, the men fought in some of the worst field conditions any army had faced. Thick forests and tangles of underbrush made it hard to move cavalry in and out of the fight. This was one battle the youngster would have to be in. He couldn't stay in camp and watch this day. Soon he was up on his horse and in the middle of the fight.

General Porter rode by at one point in the battle and caught a glimpse of the boy charging and yelling and slashing his sword at the Rebels with the fury of a man twice his age.

THWACK!

The general jumped from his chair in the hotel. He turned and glared toward the sound. It was only the waiter. He had dropped a plate into the dirty dishpan and had scurried off to the kitchen.

"Yes," the general sighed, slowly sitting back down in his corner chair. "Yes . . . he was shot in the neck by a minié ball. I couldn't get to him. Too many trees and brush and bullets flying all around, galloping horses, swords flashing from all directions. I couldn't get to him," he remembered out loud.

The boy tumbled out of the saddle and onto the forest floor. Horses thrashed over and above him. More riders came. Rebel cavalry. Union cavalry. Riderless horses that belonged to dead men.

He saw only the boy's horse, now on top of its master. Suddenly, bullets crossed the brim of the general's hat.

"I couldn't stay there. I couldn't help him. He was dead. He must have been dead. Bullet in the neck . . . horse as a coffin lid. Dead."

General Porter, now comfortable in the hotel, thought back to the talk around the campfire the night after that terrible fight. He remembered the men had heard that the name Chickamauga came from the Cherokee Indian name for the creek. It meant "river of death."

Just as he was about to get up from his hotel chair and confront this ghost from the past, he heard the gentleman's voice. The man had been watching the general from the lobby and was now standing in the dining room entrance.

"Hi, General Porter," he said, smiling. "Trying to remember me? I remember you. That was a mighty rough fight we were in. My poor little pony had half a dozen bullets in her. If she hadn't fallen on me, well . . . " he hesitated.

The general blinked and said, "Is it really you, son? How did you live through that fight? Tell me . . . please."

"Well, I lay there thinking I really was dead. My pony had me pinned, but its body protected me from any more damage. Only thing was, I couldn't get out after the shooting stopped. Thank goodness, an army surgeon came riding up and saw my hand moving under my pony's front leg. He pulled me out, took me back to a field hospital, and when I came to, I couldn't remember who I was. I was in a different brigade camp and no one recognized me. For two years I stayed in a fog. But one morning, I opened my eyes and announced to everyone in the hospital who I was!" he explained while rubbing a deep groove in his neck. "And here we are, 20 years later. My, my. Strange turn of events, wouldn't you say, General?"

General Porter was speechless. Just as the general dipped his head, grabbed the sides of the chair, and pushed back to stand and walk toward the gentleman, he was gone!

"What is your name?" the general shouted. His eyes scanned the empty hotel lobby, frantically searching for the man. "You never told me your name!"

"Beg your pardon, sir?" asked the startled waiter, who had just come back into the dining room from the kitchen.

"Never mind," said the general. "I was just talking to myself, I guess, remembering a boy—rather—a man—from the past."

A Cool-Headed Virginia Lady

⭐

Benjamin and Addie Belcher lived on a quiet little farm in the heart of Virginia. Their only son had been working in Ohio when the Civil War started and was drafted into the Union army. With both armies fighting around them, they were at the mercy of both Union and Confederate deserters or ruffians who wandered by.

One afternoon, four Union soldiers rode up to the Belchers' front porch. They jumped off their horses, ran up to Benjamin, and started yelling at him to bring all of his gold, jewelry, money, or anything valuable to them at once.

He insisted he owned nothing of any value. He didn't have any gold or jewelry and begged them to leave. They didn't believe him.

Suddenly, one of the soldiers grabbed a rope from his saddle, threw one end over the limb of a big apple tree, and told the other soldiers to hold Benjamin. The soldier then tied the other end of the rope around Benjamin's neck and pulled him toward the tree.

The soldiers took turns pulling poor Benjamin up until his feet cleared the ground. Up and down he went.

The men held him until he gasped for air, then lowered him and asked again for his valuables.

Addie was frantic. She watched the scene from her kitchen window and had remained silent for fear of what the men might do to her. After Benjamin went up for the third time, she could stand it no longer. She had to do something.

Not uttering a word, she opened the kitchen door and marched straight to the apple tree. She never missed a step or slowed her pace. She walked right between the men and stood face to face with Benjamin.

He stood there gasping for air, half alive, staring back at her. In a calm, soft, loving voice, Addie said, "Benjamin, dinner is ready."

Glancing from man to man, she turned to the Yankee ruffians and said in the same loving voice, "We would be much obliged if you would have dinner with us too."

The four Yankee soldiers were so surprised by her words, they let Benjamin down—took the rope from around his neck—and calmly walked into the kitchen and sat down for dinner.

A good home-cooked dinner could take the place of a hanging, any day!

They ate until they couldn't eat anymore, saddled up, and rode off into the sunset—never to be seen by the Belchers again.

THEIR FAITHFUL DOG

★

The Battle of Shiloh brought 40,000 Confederate soldiers and over 60,000 Union soldiers together for two days of fierce fighting.

When the battle started, wounded Union soldiers were brought to a makeshift hospital area at Pittsburg Landing, a steamer stop on the Tennessee River. Soon there were thousands of dead and dying men scattered so far apart, the doctors couldn't tend to them. They realized something new had to be tried—something that had never been done before—a "tent hospital" had to be established.

Unfortunately, even the best of tent hospitals and new ideas weren't enough to save all of the soldiers. Among the 24,000 who were killed and wounded at Shiloh was a young Union officer who had joined the fight shortly after his wedding.

He promised his new bride he would try to stay safe and well. She worried something might happen to him and insisted he take their little dog with him for protection and company on his long march from home.

The young couple would never know what an important role their faithful dog would play in the terrible days to come.

The hospital attendant tried to be polite, but he knew he wasn't doing a very good job of explaining his situation to the distraught lady: "Ma'am, I'm sorry, but I don't know where your husband is," his voice rising as he faced Mrs. Pheff.

"You don't understand, Sergeant," she pleaded, "I received this telegram saying my husband, Lieutenant Pheff, was wounded on the first day of battle—April the sixth, 1862, at Shiloh. Is this Shiloh?"

"Yes, Ma'am . . . well, sort of . . . you're at Pittsburg Landing. And this is the Union Hospital Camp. What did you say your name was again? I've got so many to keep track of. You shouldn't have come, Ma'am. This is no place for a young woman like yourself. Why, we're still burying men. We've got so many dead . . . "

The sergeant suddenly stopped talking. He was staring at the young bride's left cheek. Two large tears were silently curving down her face to the corner of her mouth.

Before he could speak again, she continued, slowly reading out loud from the telegram she held in her shaking hands.

" . . . Was wounded on the first day of battle, April the sixth, 1862, at Shiloh. Lieutenant Pheff was quickly lifted up by his men and was being rushed to the United States Army Tent Hospital when he died on the battlefield."

As she finished reading, one of the tears fell on the word *Shiloh*. The sergeant lowered his head, and without saying another word, reached for her arm. He turned her gently and walked her a few steps to a point where they could see out over the camp. He turned her again, and pointed up to a high bluff overlooking the Tennessee River.

"There," he said, "there is where your man is, Mrs. Pheff. If he died on the sixth, your lieutenant that is, if he got buried, well, there are over 3,000 men buried up there, and we only know who about a thousand are. At least 2,000 of those poor fellows will lie in unmarked graves. Your husband is probably one of them. I'm the one who marked the names, and as far as I can think back, he wasn't one of them."

She let out a small cry and sank to her knees. But as she did, she heard a familiar sound.

"Ruff! RRRRuff!" It was her husband's dog! He came running down the path from the high bluff over the landing, barking and yelping all the way. He jumped on the back of her long dress and started pulling with such a force, she stood up and tried to shake him off.

"Where have you come from?" she cried. "Look at you—all covered with dust and dirt." She reached around to pet him but quickly pulled her hand back at the sound of a low growl.

The sergeant stepped up and tried to pull the dog away, but the dog had too tight a grip on her dress. The little dog snarled and pulled and tried his best to drag her toward the bluff.

She had never seen the dog act like this.

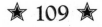

"Something is wrong. Something is very wrong, Sergeant," she said, trying to free herself.

The dog kept pulling and snarling, and only at the sight of two privates running up from behind did it let go. It barked for a moment, then ran a few feet toward the bluff. It quickly turned back to look at the startled group, and then stretched out on its stomach, never taking its eyes off Mrs. Pheff.

The sergeant demanded to know how the sight of the two of them made the dog let loose of the dress and settle down.

"That's the lieutenant's dog!" said one of the men. "Are you the lieutenant's bride?"

"Of course she is!" said the other man. "We've been watchin' out for this little fella," he said as he bent over, motioning for the dog to come to him. "Can't get him to eat, though. He keeps lookin' at every lady who comes into camp."

"Your husband sure loved that dog, Ma'am," said the first private. "Those two were never apart. The day the lieutenant . . . I mean, your husband, Lieutenant Pheff, was wounded, that dog was right there next to him in the thick of the fightin', licking his face. We got to him quick as we could, but he was hurt so bad . . . well, picked him up gentle, and that dog just went to snarlin' and barkin' so, we had to set the stretcher down. Well, Ma'am, he just hopped up on that stretcher, right next to the lieutenant, and settled down, nice and quiet. The lieutenant, he got awful quiet too. Seemed at peace, I think.

"Well, we tried to get him back as quick as we could, bullets flying and all, pretty bad day that was. But he'd passed on by the time the surgeons got to him. We buried him up on the bluff, like all the others, but with so many up there, well, Ma'am . . . there's no marker. And, the worst of it is, I can't remember just . . . "

The dog ran up to her, grabbed the end of her skirt with its mouth, and started pulling her dress with all its might. "No, Sergeant, leave him alone," she said as the sergeant stepped up to pull the dog away. She let the dog pull her along through the hospital tents and up on the path that led to the bluff. The sergeant and the two soldiers followed close behind.

Up, up, higher and higher, till they were standing on the bluff overlooking the Tennessee River on one side and row upon row of freshly dug dirt mounds on the other.

The dog suddenly let go of her dress and bolted out over the graveyard. They all followed, trying to keep the dog in sight, while running as fast as they could over the rough ground, trying not to step on the mounds where the dead soldiers lay.

At last the dog stopped at the end of one of the graves. He lowered his head, crept on his belly toward the head of the grave, quietly turned around, and waited for them to come.

"My husband! I know it's my husband. Please! Please! I must see him one last time. Let me make sure!" she begged the men as she came running up to the side of the mound.

The three men quickly fell to their knees and started digging into the mound. The dog stood up, slowly walked to the end, sat down, and patiently waited. Waited as it had since the day the lieutenant was buried there.

When they opened the coffin lid, the dog got up and walked to his lady's feet. He gently tugged once on her long skirt, curled up beside her, and slept for the first time in 12 days.

A SHARE OF SOAP

★

Private Bob was a good soldier. In fact, everyone in his regiment thought he was one of the kindest, most respectful fellows who ever wore a uniform.

He had just one peculiar habit. Everywhere the regiment went, Private Bob would march at the head of the column, scouting for a stream or river where he could take a daily bath. He would march and shout to all within range, "Cleanliness is next to Godliness!"

Every time the regiment set up a new camp, Private Bob would finish his chores and run to the stream, soap bar in hand, jump in, and take a long, refreshing bath.

Now, Private Bob really didn't bother anyone when he did this, and most of his fellow soldiers admired his desire to stay clean. Besides that, they all agreed he was the best-smelling fellow in the whole Army of Northern Virginia!

Everything was going along well for Private Bob until the day he ran out of soap. He rushed from tent to tent, asking if he could borrow a small piece of soap.

"Soap! I need soap!" he cried as he ran through the camp. "Please, fellows, can't anyone spare a bar or a scoop of soap? Doesn't anyone in this outfit know how to make a bucket of soap? HELP! I must have a bath, and I must use soap!"

Suddenly, he found himself standing next to the general's tent, where a supply wagon was sitting. The wagon was piled high with medical equipment, blankets, barrels of hardtack—and what's this? Sitting on the ground next to one of the wagon wheels—soap! A bucket of soft soap!

"One of the medical attendants must have made a fresh batch for the hospital!" Bob squealed to himself, trying not to arouse the general.

Private Bob was so excited, he grabbed the bucket and raced back through camp to the stream.

"They won't miss this small bucket," he thought to himself as he was unbuttoning his shirt on the run, "And I don't think it is really stealing. I'm sure my fellow soldiers would want me to stay smelling fresh."

At last he reached the stream bank. He pulled off his dusty uniform, threw his drawers high into the air, stuck both hands deep into the bucket, smeared a great glob on his chest, and plunged into the water!

No sooner had he made a splash than a long, sad frown covered his face. He slowly started to stand, but before he was waist high in the water, a bunch of his fellow soldiers started calling to him from the creek bank.

"Hey, Bob! Where did you get the soap? Give us some too!"

"Don't be a hog, Bob. Share with your buddies."

"Yeah! Share with your buddies."

Private Bob just stood there for a long moment. With his naked back to his friends he said, "Oh, all right. I suppose you can have a share, but just don't use it all. Remember, just don't use it ALL."

Before they even knew what was happening, Private Bob was up, out of the water, on the bank, and running—in his birthday suit—back to camp, as fast as a cat after a mouse!

He was halfway through camp, when he heard the sounds of his friends shouting, laughing and jeering, and chasing after him. Everyone in camp was stirred by this time—all laughing hysterically at the scene.

Private Bob was being chased by the half-dressed men, who had large, greasy beads of water standing out like bubbles all over their heads and shoulders. And, come to think of it, so did Bob!

It seems Private Bob had stolen a bucket of wagon wheel grease instead of a bucket of soft soap.

If that herd of fellow bathers ever caught him, they would make sure Private Bob was "squeaky" clean from that day on!

CHAMPION OF THE CAMPFIRE STORYTELLERS

★

After long days of drilling or fighting, and as a way to ease homesickness, Civil War soldiers sometimes relaxed by sitting around campfires, listening to tall tales and exciting stories told by fellow soldiers late into the night.

By the end of the war, some of the best storytellers went back home and began to publish their tallest tales for their grandchildren to read. Many of the stories gave a good picture of what life was like for the common soldier. But there were a few tall tales that were told and written for the pure fun of seeing how funny and wild a story could get.

This "true" tale was told around a campfire late one night by a young soldier who found out a new storyteller was in camp. After all, the teller of this tale was the champion of his regiment's storytellers—the best of the tall-tale spinners. He had to come up with the greatest story of all to keep his title—and to keep his audience entertained.

The angels above were all around me that day, I tell you, boys. That's the only thing I figure saved me, angels from above. Sent to guide a poor weary soldier. *Guide* is the word I want you to remember!

I was so tired of drillin' that morning. Drill, drill, drill. That's all we was doin'. Why, we drilled after hardtack breakfast, then drilled some more. Then we took the manual o' arms and drilled some more. Then we listened to that cranky sergeant scream at us and drilled some MORE! I tell you I was SICK of drilling.

Right in the middle of all the screaming, I happen to glance over the sergeant's right shoulder and I see this inviting shady spot, a soft emerald carpet of grass under a spreading oak, just a-callin' my name.

"Come and rest a spell, James. Come and rest a while," it whispered. "Come, James. Come, James."

I tell you it was a-callin' me like a sweet angel's voice from Heaven. It swept over my drillin' body till I couldn't resist anymore.

I just sorta floated toward that tree, dropped my musket on that piece of carpet, stretched my aching body out like a hunk of dough on a flour board, and closed my eyes.

AHHH . . . 'twas peaceful, for about one minute. That darn sergeant came a-stompin' up and broke my sweet spell.

"I've had it with you, James! All you think about is sleep. Up on your feet! You are in trouble this time, mister. We'll see what the colonel has to say about your little nap!"

Well, he marched me right into the colonel's tent without a-knockin' on the wood pole holdin' the flap, and guess what the colonel was a-doin'? He was sleepin' too!

He didn't much like seein' us standing there, 'cuz he must have been in the middle of an important military dream. He fussed at that sergeant, and then he would go to fussin' at me. I couldn't tell which of us was in more trouble. But it didn't take long till he told that sergeant to do what he wanted with me and not to bother him again.

Now, boys, I didn't figure that colonel was goin' to do much to me, maybe make me clean up after his horse for a day or two, but the sergeant—now, he was a different matter.

He marched me to the gunner and called for a full cannon crew. "Gunner, prepare your largest cannon. No cannon balls needed. We are about to launch an attack upon the enemy camp with a special load!"

He glared at me wickedly. I couldn't believe it! He was gonna fire me from a cannon! Now, I heard tell of another poor soul who got this treatment for doin' much worse than sleepin', and I stood there tryin' to remember just what he did to survive the firin'. While the gunner and his crew were scramblin' around and a-settin' that cannon and bringin' a bucket of gunpowder up to my feet, my mind was a-racin' about just what it was that fellow came up with to survive the flight.

"Do you have any last words, sleepyhead?" grinned that sergeant. "If I can't make a soldier out of you, then I think the least we can do is put your BODY to good use. Just imagine, you have a chance to fight and lie down while doing it . . . just what you do best!" he roared.

Just as they was about to pick me up and stick me feet first inside that black tube, it came to me! I remembered what that fellow did. I told that sergeant, seein' as how I'm a-gonna give my body to the Cause, I think I would fly faster and straighter and do more damage if he stuck me in headfirst. I could kick them guys when I land, have some extra fight left in me, so to speak.

He rubbed his chin, thought a second (probably at the picture of me flyin' into the line, a-kickin' all the way), and agreed.

The crew poured that powder down in the barrel, and in I went! It was mighty dark in there. But I went right to work. I remembered how that fellow said if you ever get put in a cannon, be sure to get 'em to load you head-first. That way you have plenty of time to EAT as much of the gunpowder as you can. The more you EAT, the softer the explosion and the cooler you'll stay!

I went to chewin' and munchin' and chewin' and swallowin' and before they lit that fuse, I had near eat up that bucket full of powder.

I dared not BURP, though. Didn't want to go off premature!

SZZZZZZZZZ. . . . The fuse was lit, and the next thing I knowed . . . KABOOM!

Boys, I was a-flyin' through the air like a minié ball headed for home. WHEEEEEEEE! The wind was blowin' through my curls, my pants legs was pushed up to my drawers, my shirt was tryin' to come off my head. Why, I must have looked like an upside-down swimmer goin' up a waterfall.

I looked back at that laughin' sergeant and couldn't hardly believe what I saw a-chasin' me! That gun crew must have had a regular cannon ball down in there that they forgot about when they loaded me!

It had shot out TOO!! It was a-flyin' at full speed and tryin' to catch up with me!

'Tweren't too awful long and here it came! I reached out and grabbed ahold with both hands and found it had HANDLES on either side. Very handy, if I say so myself.

I turned my body around and was a-sittin' on top of the thing, just a-flyin' along through space, as pretty as you please.

Now, the trip went well, till I was out of sight of my regiment. I cleared the colonel's tent, sailed over the kitchen, stables, hospital, and outhouses, when I suddenly realized I was headed straight for the enemy cavalry line.

There they was, all lined up so nice and pretty. But the wind changed, and I started to drift to the left. If I kept on a-goin' in that direction, I weren't gonna do no damage to that line. I had to do somethin' quick, or that sergeant would come after me and surely shoot me off again.

I started to wiggle and waggle and scooch that ball under me, till I got it to change direction and steered it to the middle of that pretty line.

I carefully guided that flying shot with a wiggle here and a waggle there, and KABOOM!

It worked! I wiped out half the enemy cavalry with one cannonball! Near on a hundred of 'em, I figure!

Now, I'm sure some of you are a-sittin' there a-wonderin' just how it came to be the ball did its damage. And I'm here tellin' my true story, alive and in fair condition and able to tell this heroic tale.

Just so happens that sweet angel voice that called to me about that oak tree on my drilling field—the one where I got caught a-nappin' and ended up in this pitiful mess to start with? Well, it called to me again. And just in the nick of time, I might add.

"Come and rest a spell, James. Come, James," it whispered to me.

I glanced over to my right, and there was ANOTHER big oak tree and ANOTHER soft emerald carpet of grass, even cooler-lookin' than the one in my own camp.

Just before I let that cannonball drop on the enemy cavalry, I stood up on top of that thing, aimed my body, and JUMPED for that oak tree at the very last second! I grabbed a strong limb of that mighty oak, swung down to that lovely callin' carpet below, and finally got my long-deserved sleep!

GLOSSARY

artillery: Cannons; the branch of the army in charge of the cannons (the three branches were artillery, infantry, and cavalry).

battery: A group of four or six cannons manned by an artillery crew of six or seven men and a gunner.

campaign: A plan of battle or attack; sometimes a plan would involve fighting in one area and take several days or weeks to complete.

Devil's Den: One of the battle sites at Gettysburg; on July 2, 1863, Confederate sharpshooters fired on Union troops from behind large boulders in this area.

Henry Hill: Also known as Henry House Hill, this was the site of the final stand against the Confederates at the Second Manassas, or Second Battle of Bull Run, in August of 1862.

minié (MIH-nee) ball: A soft lead ball, often called a bullet, that was loaded and fired from a Civil War rifle musket.

Napoleon (12-pounder): The most common cannon used by Civil War artillery; it could fire solid shot, case shot, shells, and cannisters two to four times a minute; it was mounted on wheels and could be pulled by a team of horses from battle to battle.

Peach Orchard: One of the battle sites at Gettysburg; on July 2, 1863, Union general Daniel Sickles and his troops fought against Confederate general Longstreet and his Rebels.

scout: A soldier or civilian who went into enemy territory or in front of advancing troops to collect information before a battle.

slouch hat: A soft leather hat that was popular with soldiers on both sides; officers wore gold cord or rope braids around the center, with insignia patches on the front for cavalry, artillery, or infantry.

telegraph: A communications system invented by Samuel Morse in 1844; a series of electric "dots" and "dashes" were sent over wires to a receiver several miles away. These signals were then translated into letters of the alphabet; an example of the help signal was dot-dot-dot, dash-dash-dash, dot-dot-dot, dash-dash-dash, sent over and over. Telegraph wagons carried sender and receiver units from battle to battle, with miles of wire strung between sites.

Wheat Field: One of the battle sites at Gettysburg; on July 2, 1863, it was fought over with neither side completely taking it.